# WILD WORK

# Who Scoops Elephant Poo?
## WORKING AT A ZOO

Margie Markarian

Chicago, Illinois

**www.heinemannraintree.com**
Visit our website to find out
more information about
Heinemann-Raintree books.

**To order:**
☎ Phone 888-454-2279
💻 Visit www.heinemannraintree.com
to browse our catalog and order online.

Edited by David Andrews, Nancy Dickmann, and Rebecca
Rissman
Designed by Victoria Allen
Picture research by Liz Alexander
Leveled by Marla Conn, with Read-Ability.
Originated by Dot Gradations Ltd
Printed and bound in China by Leo Paper Products Ltd

15 14 13 12 11 10
10 9 8 7 6 5 4 3 2 1

**Library of Congress Cataloging-in-Publication Data**
Markarian, Margie.
  Who scoops elephant poo? : working at a zoo / Margie
Markarian.
    p. cm.—(Wild work)
  Includes bibliographical references and index.
  ISBN 978-1-4109-3848-0 (hc)—ISBN 978-1-4109-3858-9
(pb)  1. Zoo animals—Juvenile literature. 2. Zoo keepers—
Juvenile literature. 3. Zoos—Employees—Juvenile literature.
4. Animal specialists—Juvenile literature.  I. Title. II. Title:
Working at a zoo.
  SF408.M37 2011
  636.088'9—dc22                           2009050279

**Acknowledgements**
The author and publisher are grateful to the following for
permission to reproduce copyright material:
© Capstone Publishers p. **11** (Karon Dubke); © Minnesota
Zoo p. **8**; Alamy pp. **4** (© Olaf Doering), **15** (© blickwinkel),
**16** (© C.O. Mercial), **20** (© Dave and Sigrun Tollerton), **23**
(© Steven May), **26** (© Bill Bachman), **27** (© Jeff Greenberg),
**28** (© Kuttig - RF – Kids); Corbis pp. **7** (© Nicky Loh/Reuters),
**17** (© Federico Gambarini), **19** (© Pavel Wolberg/epa); Getty
Images pp. **12** (Peter Macdiarmid), **14** (William West/AFP),
**18** (Jessie Cohen/Smithsonian National Zoo), **21** (WireImage),
**22** (Christopher Hunt), **29** (Thinkstock); Photolibrary pp. **5**
(Jochen Tack/imagebroker.net), **13** (Jochen Tack/imagebroker.
net), **24** (Michael DeYoung/Alaskastock), **25** (TAO Images
Limited); Rex Features p. **6** (Andrew Price); Shutterstock
pp. **9** (© G. Campbell), **10** (© ivylingpy).

Background design features reproduced with permission of
Shutterstock (© Vard). Cover photograph reproduced with
permission of Shutterstock (© Galyna Andrushko).

Every effort has been made to contact copyright holders of
any material reproduced in this book. Any omissions will
be rectified in subsequent printings if notice is given to
the publisher.

**Disclaimer**
All the Internet addresses (URLs) given in this book were valid
at the time of going to press. However, due to the dynamic
nature of the Internet, some addresses may have changed, or
sites may have changed or ceased to exist since publication.
While the author and publisher regret any inconvenience this
may cause readers, no responsibility for any such changes can
be accepted by either the author or the publisher.

Some words are shown in bold, **like this**. You can find
out what they mean by looking in the glossary.

# Contents

# Wild about Animals

People who work at zoos are wild about animals. They hang out with monkeys. They get cozy with giraffes. Sometimes, they swim with sharks. But that's not all they do!

## DID YOU KNOW?

The world's first public zoo was set up around 1470 B.C.E. in Ancient Egypt.

# Collecting Creatures

It takes a team of people to run a zoo. Head **curators** (say *cue-RAY-tors*) lead the team. They decide which animals will live in the zoo.

Some zoos let you see animals up close.

**DID YOU KNOW?**
Curators work to save
**endangered species**.
They give them homes
and encourage them
to have babies.

They create rules about animal
care, train the other zoo workers,
and help design **exhibits**.

# Building Home Sweet Home

**Exhibit** designers create living spaces for zoo animals. They try to copy the animal's natural **habitat**. This helps keep the animals happy and healthy.

Exhibit designers have given this bear rocks and logs to climb on, and water to splash in.

# The Green Team

Pandas eat bamboo. Giraffes chomp on leaves. Zebras chew on grass. **Horticulturists** (say *HOR-tuh-CUL-chure-ists*) are plant scientists. They make sure zoo animals have the trees, bushes, grasses, and other plants they need.

Horticulturists create areas that look good and are full of good things to eat!

# Who Feeds the Llamas Lunch?

Zookeepers take care of the animals. They fix meals and set out the food. They keep track of how much the animals eat.

Zookeepers check on the animals every morning and make sure they are safe at night. They understand and respect animals.

# Who Scoops Elephant Poo?

Cleaning up after animals is a stinky job, but zookeepers don't mind. They hose down hippos. They brush sea lion teeth! They even scoop elephant poo!

sea lion

**DID YOU KNOW?**
Elephant poo can be **recycled** and made into paper products.

# Open Up and Say Aaah!

What happens when a gorilla has stomach pain or a leopard cuts its paw? The zoo's medical team comes to the rescue!

**Veterinarians** are zoo doctors. They take care of animals when they are sick, hurt, or having babies.

When an animal needs an **operation** or gives birth, **veterinary technicians** help the doctor. They comfort the animal.

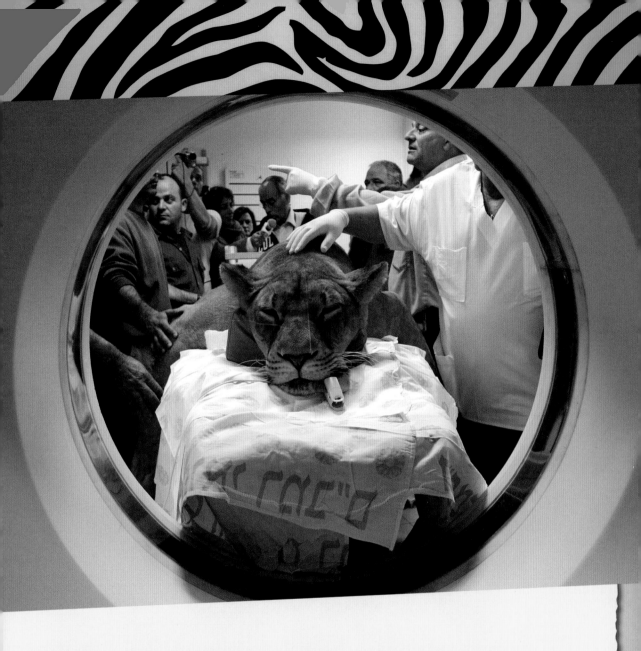

Veterinary technicians also give shots, wrap broken bones, and take temperatures. Sometimes they even give them x-rays!

# Just Call Me Coach

This koala looks cute and cuddly. But it's still a wild animal! Animal handlers understand how animals act. They teach them to follow directions and do tricks. The job takes time, patience, and kindness.

## DID YOU KNOW?

Many animal handlers got their start as kids training their pets or farm animals.

# What's the Buzz?

Bugs are part of the animal world too. **Entomologists** (say *EN-tome-OL-oh-jists*) create zoo **exhibits** starring chirping crickets and beautiful butterflies. They are scientists who study bugs. Spider experts show visitors hairy tarantulas.

## DID YOU KNOW?

Tarantulas don't usually bother humans. A tarantula bite is like a bee sting. It hurts, but it's not deadly unless you are **allergic**.

tarantula

# Flipping for Fins

Some zoos are homes to sea creatures. **Aquarists** (say *ah-KWAR-ists*) take care of fish and other sea animals. They check the tank water and make sure it's the right temperature. They dive in deep to clean the tanks. They care for plants and even feed hungry sharks!

# Teaching Others

Zoo educators share their love and knowledge of animals with visitors. They lead tours and hold show and tell programs. Sometimes they appear on TV and visit with school groups. They enjoy being with animals and talking to people.

# Could You Work at a Zoo?

If you love working with all kinds of animals, you could have a zoo career. But the jobs are hard to get!

It helps to study animal science in school. You can also get experience working with animals. Caring for pets or farm animals, or working at an animal shelter, can help you get a job at a zoo.

# Glossary

**allergic** being sensitive to some plants, animals, or materials. Allergies can make some people sick.

**aquarist** a person who cares for fish and other sea creatures

**curator** a person who takes care of animal exhibits at a zoo or objects in collections at museums

**endangered species** type of animal in danger of dying out

**entomologist** a scientist who studies insects and spiders

**exhibits** displays at zoos or museums

**habitat** the natural home of an animal

**horticulturist** a scientist who studies plants

**operation** something done inside the body to help humans and other animals. Doctors and veterinatians do operations.

**recycle** use again in another form

**veterinarian** a doctor who takes care of animals

**veterinary technician** a person who assists a veterinarian (animal doctor)

# Find Out More

## Books to Read

Arlon, Penelope. *DK First Animal Encyclopedia*, New York: Dorling Kindersley Limited, 2004.

The San Diego Zoo. *My Big Book of Wild Animals*. Nashville, TN: Ideals Children's Book, 2007.

McGhee, Karen and George McKay. *Encyclopedia of Animals*, Washington, DC: National Geographic Children's Books, 2007.

## Web Sites to Visit

**http://www.sandiegozoo.org/kids/job_profiles.html**
Get more exciting details on zoo careers from experts at the San Diego Zoo.

**http://kids.nationalgeographic.com/Animals**
Fun facts and photos about dozens of amazing wild animals and their habitats.

**http://animal.discovery.com/guides/endangered/endangered.html**
From giant armadillos to snow leopards, learn about some of the world's most endangered species.

# Index